Shut Up, Helen

Helen Rose

Mokwa's Peacock
Publishing

The opinions expressed in this manuscript are solely the opinions of the author and do not represent the opinions or thoughts of the publisher. The author has represented and warranted full ownership and/or legal right to publish all the materials in this book.

Shut Up Helen
All Rights Reserved.
Copyright © 2015 Helen Rose
v2.0

Cover Photo © 2015 Johnna Filipkowski Vona. All rights reserved - used with permission.

This book may not be reproduced, transmitted, or stored in whole or in part by any means, including graphic, electronic, or mechanical without the express written consent of the publisher except in the case of brief quotations embodied in critical articles and reviews.

Mokwa's Peacock Publishing

ISBN: 978-0-578-16240-9

Outskirts Press and the "OP" logo are trademarks belonging to Outskirts Press, Inc.

PRINTED IN THE UNITED STATES OF AMERICA

DEDICATED TO:

All the people, who have been injured at work or other and have had to deal with Insurance Carriers > Compensation / No-Fault, etc....like myself. Also, praises to the Erin Brockovich's of the world......

Also dedicated to the memory of my late Mother who always aspired me with a fabulous outlook of life that no matter what> to be positive/optimistic NOT negative/pessimistic. She always told me > nobody loves you as much as your mother does, and she was right!

Last but not least, dedicated also to my late father who was the joy of my world......I lost him to cancer when I was nineteen years old and pregnant with my second daughter Laurie. His philosophy was if you can't say something nice about someone, never say anything at all!

Love you both Dad & Mom, xoxoxoxo until we meet again.

I truly understand the position of the insurance carriers, especially the compensation carriers and would not want to be in their shoes to sort out the fakes from the workers who are really hurt!

I understand the frustration, the feelings of helplessness and depression that goes along with being out of work for a significant amount of time.

I also can relate to the grueling therapy, which no matter how hard we try doesn't just give us, a quick fix!

I also want to thank my friends and family, especially my youngest daughter Johnna, for much desired / needed help and support with these touchy issues……

As this is actually a true personal story of mine, I tried to make a short story and humorously written, so I wouldn't bore anyone to death on this subject, come to think of it now, it is actually quite funny to most who have read my script.

Ironically……Some names have been changed to protect the "GUILTY"

CONTENTS

Chapter 1	The Nightmare Begins Year-1999	1
Chapter 2	Doctor & MRI	3
Chapter 3	Lawyer Hunt	6
Chapter 4	Surgery/August 1999	8
Chapter 5	Therapy-September 1999	9
Chapter 6	Senator & Court February 2000	13
Chapter 7	Manipulation & Late Checks January 1999-May 2000	15
Chapter 8	Second Lawyer	16
Chapter 9	Land Therapy Again	18
Chapter 10	Lawyers Galore >>>>Old Saying… when it rains--it pours	20
Chapter 11	Out of Town Relief?	25
Chapter 12	Court……The Fiasco/Joke	27
Chapter 13	Second Car Accident	29
Epilogue		30

CHAPTER 1

THE NIGHTMARE BEGINS YEAR-1999

"What do you mean; I can't have my check until I have an MRI scheduled and all my medicals sent to you directly?" "I have bills; an apartment with the rent due NOW, it has been nine weeks without a paycheck!" "It is your job to request my medicals from the doctor's, etc., you're the so-called professional!" "The MRI isn't possible till sometime next week," replied the carrier.

This was only the beginning of what I was about to experience for the next umpteen years, clearly an insurance nightmare.

The story unfolds on April 12, 1999; I had risen early, 4:00 a.m., my usual to get ready for my day, my full time job (retail accountant-40 hrs.). When I was done there, I'd head out to my part-time job (cosmetician-20 hrs.) for one of the beauty lines here in town. I had originally worked full-time as a sales associate for one of the stores in town. Retail doesn't pay very much, so I needed to work part time too. I was new to the job market, suddenly supplying for myself after raising four daughters and taking care of my elderly mother who lived with me and my family for 30 years plus, since my dad died in 1968. I was used to being very active and busy, not only taking care of my family, but also doing odd jobs of cleaning private homes for extra pocket money, which I loved! This job hunting was quite a challenge, as I had no college education. I had just received my GED, thirty years after the fact. I was computer illiterate, better word> computer stupid, I didn't even know how to turn a computer on! Actually, typing was one of my majors in high school, but the old saying proved true, "if you don't use it, you'll lose it".

An acquaintance of mine told me his company was hiring for a retail accounting position. I laughed. Oh, what he didn't know! He had a computer brain and a Master's Degree in Accounting! Well, at one time, a long time ago, I was very good in math (star pupil in Algebra). I also reasoned, I knew how to add my bills, I had enough of them. I thanked him and applied for the job, and you guessed it, they actually hired me! Ha!

I started the first position as a warehouse retail accountant for a couple of months, then a DSD clerk (I still don't know what that is??) for a few more months. I had befriended a girl named Rosemary who took me under her wing from day one. She told me there was an opening in her department, which supposedly was not as difficult as I was doing. So I took the new position (officially now I was called "The Wic Girl"), however, now I was required at the end of the day to lift boxes containing checks (six boxes in all>around 10 to 12 pounds in weight a-piece) and was required to put them away in the manager's office for safekeeping.

Well, on that awful day, April 12, 1999, when I lifted a box of those checks, I felt a twinge, actually a shooting pain steadily increasing in the middle of my left knee which changed my life forever>>>> However, at this time I didn't know it yet! I went home that day from work at my first job, pain steadily increasing with noticeable swelling. I didn't even go to my second job. Now you have to realize, I NEVER took a day off from work. I called my boss at my second job and told them I was hurt at work and was seeing the doctor tomorrow.

CHAPTER 2

DOCTOR & MRI

I went into the doctor's office not knowing what I was going to hear. I reasoned with myself, how bad could this be Helen? You probably pulled something in your knee, the doctor will give you something for pain and tell you not to do too much work and take it easy for a couple of days, also! Right? Wrong!!!!!

"Hi Helen! What brings you here today"? "Well, Dr. C., I hurt myself at work and my left knee is killing me! I'm sure, it's probably nothing serious at all, (I couldn't afford for it to be serious, and I was too busy"!) The kind doctor said let me take a look, so he touched my knee at different places and then he hit it! "Oww, that hurts." "Well Helen, I think you've torn your meniscus." "I said, tore my what?" "Your meniscus! That is another name for the cartilage in your knee." "I think you should go to therapy to see if that will correct the problem and pain." "We'll send you to a therapy office in your area, okay?" "You were hurt at work, and with an all-knowing shake of the head, "Welcome to the World of Compensation." "I'll have to send for an authorization for therapy to your place of employment which they'll send to their insurance company."

So I started therapy almost immediately within the next couple of days. I never realized therapy could be so, so, painful, this meniscus thing was quite a trip. Mind you, I wasn't your typical cry-baby or wimp. I also was your typical tomboy teenager, Miss Daredevil Herself!!!!! As a child, I was the only kid in the doctor's office who would rather have a shot in the arm or elsewhere instead of a pill! I also had my share of surgeries, two major and a number of minor, one miscarriage with five pregnancies and major dental work in my teens, twenties, thirties, forties, and fifties,

And beyond……

I returned to my doctor with no improvement, so now, he tells me to baby my knee while we are waiting for the insurance carrier to approve the MRI.

SEVEN WEEKS have gone by now…… NO check and NO MRI approval! So, I call the carrier. "Ms. Star, this is Helen Rose, I was calling regarding my check and my MRI." "Well, I have been looking to get you into a "SPECIFIC" IME/Compensation Doctor (I had no idea what IME meant, but I have some choice words for that phrase/type of doctor now, as I have seen my share> now remember these doctors are paid by the insurance carrier), but they can't get you in for a couple of weeks, so I can't send out your check yet!" "Sorrrrrry!" "My Doctor is looking to have me checked for phlebitis to make sure it's not my vein, I said." "Well, if that is the case, we'll have to wait for that report, she said." I thought to myself, Helen that was a stupid statement to tell this woman who had control of your check! "I sure hope that you send my check soon, my rent is/was due, I could use some groceries and my bills will be paid late, so there goes my excellent credit standing!" "I hope you don't mind if I move in with you, when I am evicted, I told the carrier!"

I called the carrier about a week and a half later and told her the vascular surgeon ruled out phlebitis, my veins were fine. So now another problem, the carrier now informs me that I have to pay for the vascular surgeon's bill because phlebitis is not work related!!!! I now told the carrier that she WOULD pay this bill, because my doctor had this test done to protect the carrier/HER. If it was phlebitis, the carrier would not have to pay anything as phlebitis is not work related....and the insurance carrier must have paid, because I never did and I never received a bill for it!

This was the end with the carrier of our talking relationship, because the finally received MRI verified a torn meniscus anciently known as a bucket tear...

So the check was finally sent out that week with extreme pressure from my wonderful employer, (this was probably because three supervisors had seen me hurt myself when I lifted that box!) THAT GLORIOUS CHECK ARRIVED NINE WEEKS AFTER THE INJURY!!!!!

The insurance company now gave me over to another gem of a person in their establishment because Ms. Star would not deal with me anymore!

CHAPTER **3**

LAWYER HUNT

Now I knew I had to hire a reputable/good lawyer! Where and how would I find one? A good one I mean, I had dealt with various lawyers throughout the years. I knew I had my work cut out for me, so I decided to call the lawyers I had dealt with in the past! I called two reputable compensation lawyers, however, when I called them and talked to them, they told me they had went over to the other side and now worked for the compensation insurance company ONLY....they were NOT for the hurt victims. They told me to look in the phone book/yellow pages under the heading Compensation Lawyers. So my hunt started and lo and behold, I found my first lawyer (a compensation miracle worker, so I thought) I was thrilled. I was home free now; this lawyer would certainly take care of all this baloney I was experiencing from this awful carrier! Little did I know what was to follow, so I called this office, his staff seemed nice enough so I made an appointment to go and see my new savior!

I walked into his office, the girl sitting at the desk said hello and took my name. This was a nice office, pleasant atmosphere. This was going to be all right! The secretary had me fill out some papers to get familiar with my case. I finished filling them out, gave them back to her. She said to me, "Helen, Mr. Sweet will be with you in a moment." I waited a few more minutes, the door opened, "Helen, I'm Mr. Sweet

LAWYER HUNT

and I'll be handling your case for this law firm." "Please step into my office and we'll discuss your case and sign the necessary papers." Now mind you, I'm the type of person who normally doesn't judge a book by its cover, I try to get to know someone first, and then I either like them or not! Why was my gut feeling telling me I should walk out now? I reasoned with myself, Helen don't jump to conclusions……. this guy is on your side remember! He was very impersonal and kind-of-bothered by my story or was I just reading into things? So after he was done interrogating me, so I felt, I signed the papers with my "new" lawyer and went home and dismissed all these crazy thoughts of mistrust>for a while anyway! How bad could he be with a name like (SWEET)?

CHAPTER **4**

SURGERY/AUGUST 1999

My surgery is finally approved after waiting for authorization from May of 1999 to August of 1999. Can you believe it took THREE months for the carrier to approve arthroscopy for my knee? Dr. C. operated on my knee and he was very concerned. I had a very large tear and he told me I should weigh 300 plus pounds for the size of this tear...... now mind you I weighed around 120 lbs.! I was pretty scared......I don't like surgery or hospitals and I've had my share!

The carrier told me a while back, when I told her I didn't want to have surgery, that if I refused surgery, my checks could be stopped! As usual, the carrier could threaten and do whatever they darned well pleased with no repercussions! It's ironic, because I was so scared that I wouldn't be able to walk on crutches. That scared me more than anything else, but I became the best crutch walker, as I was on a single crutch for around 6 years plus. I could not use a cane because when I tried a cane my back would go out! I got through surgery, now my life would be starting to come together or so I thought! My lawyer was in control, everything would be okay and I would be back to work soon. On to Therapy!

CHAPTER **5**

THERAPY-SEPTEMBER 1999

"Hi! My name is Helen; I have an appointment this morning for therapy with Stacy." "I had surgery three days ago and I guess this is going to be three times a week for land therapy." "Okay Helen, take a seat and the therapist will be right with you." I hobbled to my seat on my crutches, before I sat down I looked at my knee which was pretty well bent, almost as bad as the shape of one of those boomerangs they use in Australia that returns to the thrower if they miss their target! Well, I sure hoped Stacy was going to straighten this boomerang leg and make it normal tike before!!

"Helen, Hi I'm Stacy." "Oh…Hi, I'm Helen, pardon my look of surprise, when they told me Stacy was my therapist, I guess I wrongly assumed you were a girl, but you're a guy!" "That's okay, it really doesn't matter." I'm sure you'll do just fine."

I followed this man into the exercise area. He was young, about late twenties and friendly! Well, he put ice on my knee/leg for about fifteen minutes and then the exercises began after he measured my leg for extension and flexion. My leg extension was 70 degrees (normal is 0) and he agreed with me that it did look like a boomerang. My leg flexion was about 85-90 degrees (normal is 145). So he started to give me exercises to improve these degrees and that was fine but painful, I knew it had to be done! Now he comes over to me and starts putting ALL HIS BODY WEIGHT on my leg to straighten it! I said, "whoa" what are you doing?" Adamantly, he says…."I'm straightening your leg." "I understand that, but I am seeing stars everything is going black." "Oh, he says that's okay we have to straighten this leg." "I understand this leg has to be straightened, but this is my first visit and I have six more weeks of therapy!!!!!!"

"Oh yeah, that's right I guess we can stop for today, we've got the leg to thirty degrees from 70 degrees from when you came in today." STOP FOR TODAY and every other day, I wasn't going back to this inflictor of pain anytime soon, I reasoned.

I went home and called my doctor's office. "Dr. C's office, please hold," I heard the secretary say. I waited, "Hello, this is Kathy, how may I direct your call?" "Hi Kathy, this is Helen Rose, I have just come back from therapy and I'm pretty upset." "The therapist took my leg from 70 degrees extension to 30 degrees in about five minutes and he just laid his whole being on my leg!" "I kept on telling the therapist that I was seeing black in front of me." "Now Kathy, don't get me wrong, I understand that my leg has to be straightened, but I didn't think this would happen ALL in ONE session." "Please ask the doctor if this is normal or am I making too much out of it?" Kathy came back a couple of minutes later. "Helen, he told me to send you to Health South, it is right in your area." "Alright, "I told her. " I'll try them, thank you."

I'm taking Johnna with me this time when these new therapists evaluate me, I reasoned! My daughter knew I wasn't happy about returning to therapy at all after the last place or episode. "Relax mom, it will be okay……they all know you are in a lot of pain, they'll be easy on you!" "Hi, I'm Brad." Oh great, this guy is bigger than the last one. He surely was going to break my leg!!! "I'm the manager here at Health South; now tell me everything about your

THERAPY-SEPTEMBER 1999

knee, leg and whatnot." I told him how rough the therapist at the former place was and he actually sympathized and understood. I started to relax; it was going to be okay! He measured my leg and did all the preliminaries. He introduced me to all the therapists who would be working with me every day......three times a week. Mark, Melanie, Heather, Karissa and April were the first ones I met. Then about a year down the road, Marybeth who took April's place came to be my main therapist along with Adrian. The whole office was absolutely very caring and understanding. I came back the next day. Brad spotted me. "Hi Helen, you came back," he said. "That's a good sign." Then he laughed!

I continued with therapy three times a week. Nobody understands what it is like to have someone or something like machines pull on your body all different ways unless you have been in therapy for an injury. It is very grueling and stressful. I worked mostly with Karissa in the clinic and she truly understood the pain I was experiencing as she had torn her meniscus once and tore her ACL twice. She was only twenty three years old at the time of her working with me! I would always tell the therapists, "I'm no spring chicken, so please be easy with me."

Well, they all worked hard with me, but to no avail....the more extension I got the less flexion I got and vice versa. I felt like I was on a merry-go-round. From September of 1999 to January of 2000 (5 months) they had me in land therapy twice a week (this means in the clinic using machines) and aquatic therapy (water/pool) once a week! I kept on telling the therapists and my doctor that I couldn't walk very well after therapy, so I was finally put into aquatic only! The water at least made the exercises more tolerable and made me feel better! Also, I wasn't able to sit down in my own bath tub---because I couldn't get back up. Stairs were also difficult to master......thank God, I didn't live in a high rise apartment.

◄ **SHUT UP HELEN**

The therapists all told me my knee was actually frozen because we couldn't get it to extend less than 16 degrees and bending only to 98 degrees. Quite a difference then when I started at seventy degrees. I felt the carrier was responsible because it took them THREE months to even approve my surgery! There is that magic Three again.

These therapists were actually helping me and were nice about it too!

CHAPTER **6**

SENATOR & COURT FEBRUARY 2000

I now sent a letter to the assemblyman of my district where I lived. He replied almost immediately. I told him I was going to court on Thursday. He was to await the outcome before he took any action!! When I arrived at the Compensation Board, my lawyer was not there as yet; eventually he arrived, also. He came over and talked to me for a few minutes literally before my name was called. My lawyer told me he had the results of my last visit to the Compensation/IME doctor and this second comp doctor said I was somewhat disabled!!! However, He took no note that I still couldn't bend or straighten my knee (frozen) too well, still on a crutch since August of 1999 on the advice of my therapists & Doctor, so I don't pull my back out, because I am now walking crooked! My doctor, Dr. C. has me Totally Disabled and requested surgery on February 4th. He and I are still waiting for an authorization. The last time I sought an approval for surgery in August 1999.... I waited THREE months for arthroscopy to be done on my knee.

BEFORE WE SAW THE JUDGE:

My comp lawyer told me the compensation carrier now wanted to LOWER my checks more, to ($88.00 per week from $150.00). Can you believe that? Also no concurrent employment in the picture!

SHUT UP HELEN

Concurrent Employment means that I had wages coming from another job because I was working two jobs at the time I was hurt and this injury put me out of my second job also. My lawyer and I-still talking-I-told-him-> I wasn't about to have surgery on $150.00 a week, let alone now $88.00 a week. I also told my lawyer that I was getting in touch with my assemblyman the moment I returned home and I was going to appear on every talk show in America to state my case!!!!! Immediately, his tone changed to much nicer and he said he would ask the judge for $208.00 per week including concurrent employment! My lawyer now drops his fee bomb for today totaling $700.00!!!!! Something is wrong here I told him, and where did he expect me to get this money?? "Helen Rose, please meet in Room 2", I heard the Judges' voice over the intercom. As my first paragraph of this chapter mentioned, your lawyer takes a lot of time with you!!!!!! Now mind you this is a comp lawyer! He's on my side, oh sure!

WITH THE JUDGE:

The Judge realized the compensation carrier was trying to push the concurrent employment under the rug again, (we've been trying to get these concurrent wages, since I went out on comp/April 1999). However, the Judge ruled for $208.00 per week and also gave me my concurrent wages retroactive from April 1999. I was too stressed and too tired by now to be thrilled.

P.S. The Judge approved my lawyer's fee of $700.00 with no objection what-so-ever, I guess my lawyer needs the money more than I do!!!!! WHAT A FAIR SYSTEM WE LIVE UNDER!

CHAPTER **7**

MANIPULATION & LATE CHECKS
JANUARY 1999-MAY 2000

The therapists and doctor now have been calling the compensation carrier to request a manipulation, because I am not getting any better, actually I was getting worse even though I was doing therapy! They started requesting the manipulation in February of 2000. THREE months after persistent calling (the number THREE must be a magic number for comp) I finally got an approval. It took three months for authorization approval the last time too!

Finally, May of 2000, I went in for surgery or manipulation under anesthesia. To manipulate the leg, they have to bend and straighten it to tear the scar tissue so the leg has mobility again! However, there is a risk of breaking the leg! I was worried about that because my batting average has not been very good lately. Well, they didn't break my leg, so I was thrilled! However, the comp carrier broke my spirit anyway, because she waited till I was down and out and in pain and held my check back for over 30 days. Her logic probably was that I couldn't move anyway, so what did I need money for??

As usual, my lawyer couldn't do a thing about it either. (Same old story)

CHAPTER **8**

SECOND LAWYER

Here we go again! My FIRST lawyer in a letter to me said, "The Board works in Mysterious Ways." I was starting to think this whole situation was pretty mysterious, as I now had decided to look for another lawyer because I didn't trust him or his advice. It was a pull teeth situation to get him or his office to call back when I needed him or had a question! So looking for lawyer number two and back to the drawing board, actually the trusted yellow pages, I started calling again...... one, two, three, four, five, six, etc. etc. etc. I called in all>around 30 or 40 lawyers in and out of town and they gave me the same story. I, even though on crutches and all, started to visit lawyers' offices and they ALL basically said the same thing. "What do you think I'm going to do for you that your present lawyer hasn't done already?" "Good Day Sir, I guess you're not the lawyer to help me." By the way, these were ALL compensation lawyers!!!! My gut feeling was starting to prove true; I felt right from day one that the compensation lawyers were all collaborating with one another. Many people had mentioned to me and who had dealt with compensation in times past told me to watch out and they called it A Big Boys Club. Now what was I going to do??

I stopped by one of the department stores to use an easy access ladies room (I knew them all by now) and as I was hobbling back to my car I

SECOND LAWYER

heard someone say, "Helen, what happened to you?' I turned around and saw my old friend Shelly, who I've known since we were teenagers. Gosh, that's a long time ago! "Hi Shelly, how have you been?' We shot the breeze for a few minutes and then I started to tell her about my dilemma. She gave me the name of a reputable lawyer (so I thought). It's my fathers' lawyer. Shelly's father was a very prominent owner of a couple of new & used car dealerships in the city and a sweetheart of a guy. So I reasoned this lawyer must be great if Shelly's father used him. He could hire anybody because he was well to do. Shelly told me to let the lawyer know her father had recommended him. I thanked her and said we would get together when I felt better.

CHAPTER 9

LAND THERAPY AGAIN......

For a few months, I was doing aquatic therapy (May- October of 2000). Now mind you the water therapy helped my knee feel better, but this wasn't good enough for the carrier. The carrier called my therapist and told her that compensation doesn't pay for maintenance (where you stay the same in degrees, I guess), however my doctor disagreed that it was only maintenance!!! It was helping me. So the carrier pushing the therapist, now decided to put me in land therapy again (remember, five months of LAND therapy made me worse the last time!!!!). I reluctantly agreed, but I wasn't going to like torturing myself for another five months! Well, Marybeth (therapist) after one month decided the land therapy was making me worse, now I really couldn't walk!!! My knee now really couldn't straighten and was oh so painful> actually worse than ever! Thanks to comp/carrier again my knee was really frozen, now!!!

Marybeth now discharged me on 12/01/00. Marybeth sent a letter to the compensation carrier telling her there was nothing more that land therapy could do! The therapist (sweet Marybeth-she knew how I was suffering) recommended aquatic therapy again and requested the comp carrier to approve a year membership at the YWCA, because the water made my knee pain problem tolerable! It's ironic that the compensation insurance companies want you to return to work ASAP, yet they hinder you in anything that helps you do just that!

It is the beginning of January 2001, the carrier finally after three months of requests has finally approved aquatic therapy for $200.00 a visit ($400.00-twice a week). I don't understand why they wouldn't approve a YWCA membership for ONE YEAR for about $500.00 yearly! It doesn't make sense to me...... maybe the carrier was afraid if I had that years' membership that I would become an Olympian Swimmer!!!! Ha!

CHAPTER **10**

LAWYERS GALORE >>>>OLD SAYING...*when it rains--it pours*

Pretty happy now! I might have a new 2nd lawyer????? I went to see my girlfriends' lawyer (Mr. V.) that she advised....He was pretty nice, very compassionate, sympathetic, understanding and he agreed to handle my case.

Well, as the title of this chapter states, *when it rains--it pours*, now, I not only had a compensation case, but a no-fault case as well, and possibly a GOOD lawyer?

On November 22, 2000, My daughter and I were heading to the mall on a dry afternoon and coming around the corner on the East Wing of the mall, a young man around 17 or 18 yrs. old, so I quickly surmised was flying right towards us and I swerved and he hit us head on into the drivers' side of our vehicle. Johnna screamed! "Watch out mom!" "I see him..." I said. I tried to swerve to the right to avoid him, but he got us good, totaled our car and almost us, sometimes I think it would have been better if he killed us for all the physical pain, mental anguish and lawyer baloney we were about to encounter with NOW the no-fault system!

LAWYERS GALORE >>>>OLD SAYING...WHEN IT RAINS--IT POURS ➤

Well, now on top of my comp injuries which affected my lower body, my knees, now I had new no-fault injuries, on my upper body which affected my arm, hands, shoulder, head/concussion, upper back and neck. Also, poor Johnna was now involved; as she was hurt big time with concussion/head, back, neck injuries and jaw problems...We had to be cut out of the car as the Paramedics thought we had broken our necks!

This lawyer, I hoped would have it all under control......Well, the first time I visited his office....I gave him copies of all my papers and he told me he would make me copies and send them to me... stupid me... I trusted him and agreed to that arrangement...well, you guessed it... I never saw my papers again and how stupid was I to give him originals instead of copies!!! I called his office numerous times and he avoided me or would let his secretary pacify me. First problem, I asked him to help me with right away was the no-fault insurance company would not give us the due compensation or worth of around $2,600.00 for our totaled car. So this lawyer started to write them letters to do so and sent me copies also, so I thought He was legit. The insurance carrier had the gall to drop the totaled vehicle in our driveway and sent us a check for $1000.00 and told us that was all they were paying us, so my lawyer said cash it. We had to get a truck company with a flatbed to remove the car and tow it away!!

Now, taken out of my comp check was $20.00 weekly for a supposed OVERPAYMENT of $1000.00 since I hired this new lawyer! Wouldn't I or you have known if someone overpaid a $1000.00? I kept on notifying this lawyer and he would send me letters that he was requesting the comp carrier to give me back this money for months.

My checks would always show a $20.00 deduction with overpayment written on my check. Finally, one day I received my check expecting overpayment written on my check, as usual and I see lawyer fee written instead. I immediately called the comp carrier and they said the normal girl who wrote the checks was sick, but it was a lawyers' fee for my new lawyer, Mr. V. I hired......so needless to say ... I fired him and looked for a new lawyer, so back to the drawing board......

What was the problem here? I didn't do anything wrong, nor did Johnna and it seemed like these lawyers were after us...I went through the yellow pages again and I found a wonderful comp lawyer, who could not take me, because of conflict of interest, but he gave me a lot of advice under the table as to what I should do. So, I hired reputable (so I thought) Lawyer # 3 compensation lawyer ONLY > MR. O. and he got my $700.00 back from the crook. He told me they were going to appeal my problem and **All** my checks would stop for about 5-6 months ...well, that happened and it was hairy for a while, no money at all coming in... I did win the Appeal, but this 3rd lawyer harassed me by phone and in writing......I contacted two-three senators in Syracuse who were in office at the time, these big name senators who would not help me gave me the run around. Many are still running for different offices this day and age.

Needless to say, I had to fire Comp-Lawyer # 3. Down the road thankfully I hired a fabulous Comp-Lawyer who to this day is still wonderful and watching over me, how, how, how did I find him and keep him? Now on to Lawyer # four for a no-fault lawyer.......I decided to call the head of a Local Union here, where I knew a fair and concise man, he started to give me lawyers' names, but as soon as they heard my last name, they would not handle my case......talk about the buddy system or liar/lawyer oath!!! This Union Rep couldn't believe it!

He finally found me Lawyer # Four, Mr. Bob. My friend of the Union told me he was the Perry Mason of the city court system----oh sure!!!! Probably for the bad guys!! That went down the tubes after a while and I now had to go out of town for another Lawyer...I must have called a million or it felt like it......lawyers. Through all this looking for lawyers, can you guess now what happened? Another car accident

LAWYERS GALORE > > > >OLD SAYING...WHEN IT RAINS--IT POURS ➤

in June of 2002, Johnna and I were rear-ended sitting stopped totally at a red-light., he was an older man who didn't realize we were stopped, hit us full force in the rear-end and threw us into the person's car in front of us >Double Whammy!!! ......Please remember these car accidents ALL 100% NOT our fault......the Judge himself in writing verified negligence!

On to Lawyer # Five---Mr. Pan, can you believe this???? I called a lawyer now who I saw won a huge settlement for a lady in the newspaper whose injuries were not as traumatic as ours even. He agreed I was getting the run around......

This lawyer was fantastic in calling me constantly, but He kept pushing me to drop/dismiss the first car case/accident??? He would call Johnna and ask her if I had certain papers or videos or pictures, because he had lost them......Johnna knew me better than anyone and knew me well, she would tell him, my mother doesn't lose anything and to this day, I still have all the copies of all the cases and info !

The big problem with the first car accident was it was a young Lawyers' son who hit us; he received three tickets that were dismissed! We kept on asking ALL our lawyers......"Who dismissed the THREE tickets and WHY?" Never got an answer to this day! His father worked for the biggest law firm in the town here... What does that tell you? Now it clicked why we were the enemies of the city!!!!! Lawyer # five finally tried to push us to the limit to dismiss the first car accident, wouldn't let us talk to the Judge and he told us if we didn't dismiss it...he was dismissing us, so I said so be it......Lawyer-less again????? Now what? Well, we appeared in court and were told by the Judge that we had to have a lawyer....bottom-line!!! Oh boy, now who and from where was I going to get another lawyer????????? Now, through all this craziness, we had made an appointment with a lawyer for another matter and as we were discussing different topics, of course our car accidents came up through his questioning and when he found out we

SHUT UP HELEN

were lawyer less, he started to drill us and he made us hire him on the spot—he was so excited that he had us coming to his daughters' wedding (good friends now we were) and he called the no-fault insurance man a NAZI and said he would take care of him!!! He wanted me to bring him copies of ALL our papers and wanted them quick! Needless to say, I stayed up most of the next three nights and got a million (it sure felt like that many?) copies ready. Well, we were pretty glad and he was too for a time, until about three days later, I dropped off the papers to him and he politely told us he could not handle our cases as there was a conflict of interest! Poor Johnna …. She was involved, not only was I her mother, but she was stuck with any lawyer I could get, she didn't know who to get either, but she tried!!! The little darling, what a fiasco, she was involved in with her crazy mother! I even contacted the local newspaper, the editor in chief would not print my story that included a lawyers' son, and he said he was afraid his paper could get sued!

I called the Broome County Lawyer Referral, and they gave me a big time lawyer out of town, so on we trekked down to his office, about a three hour drive, pretty far especially for us. Johnna and I were not world travelers, we could get lost in town, but we had no choice……I can't believe our SIXTH lawyer!!!

CHAPTER **11**

OUT OF TOWN RELIEF?

Johnna and I found the lawyer's office okay thanks to the secretary's directions……actually it was quite easy once we got off the super highway. The secretary was actually the lawyer's wife named Ann, it was family owned with two sons' that were lawyers under their father. The office was very elaborate / ritzy. I had actually called to see if I had a malpractice case against the lawyer who threatened me in writing and harassed me by phone.

I saw the father of the firm and he was bold and told me no lawyer would sue another lawyer for legal malpractice, at least not anyone around here. He was very gruff and kinda scary, so I reasoned he probably would do well in court if need be. He asked me if I had lawyer representation now and if not said he would be willing to take us on for our two car accidents. I thanked him after about 30 minutes of talking and we left. We never signed papers that day, so did we have a lawyer or not??? Time did tell!

Eventually, I received a letter from the court, so I had to see if we were going to be signed on with this new lawyer number SIX? I called their office and talked with the secretary/mother/Ann again and she made an appointment for us to come down and sign the papers.

Well, at least I think we have a lawyer……we walked into the office…. the whole family was extremely nice, the sisters were secretaries also there and our lawyer would not be the father, it would be the son, Matt. A real likable young fellow and he told me that he would have done everything I did to get to this point….so that made us feel better. He signed us up, so we really do have a lawyer, for how long???? Who knows????

In time, Matt told us we were going to court for the first car accident and he NEVER asked us to dismiss it?? Probably knew, I was going to fight tooth and nail for that point!

CHAPTER **12**

COURT......THE FIASCO/JOKE

Matt (Our Lawyer) met us that morning at the County Court House in our town. I would have preferred to take this case out of town also due to the circumstances of a local lawyer's son's involvement. I asked for that right at the beginning of discussion, but I was told you had to be heard in your locality. Matt said it would probably be a 4-5 day session.

Matt proceeded down the hall to the Judge's Chambers and came back pretty quickly and told us the lawyer's son who hit us and was the GUILTY STAR of this whole problem couldn't make court>unknown reason? I told Matt then we are leaving. He said, "Helen if you walk, then I won't represent you ....we are done!" Oh great.... I wish I did walk at that time, but I had no choice because they probably would have dismissed the case and thrown the whole law suit out and Johnna and I would have been up the creek......

Another problem was the original Judge was not there either....the one who right from the beginning seemed fair! The Opposing Insurance Attorney who was fighting us from day one walked in with the lawyer's son's mother Ann. We probably would have never known who she was unless we asked? That we did! She sat where her son should have been sitting! Johnna and I with the help of our lawyer got to pick the jury,,,,,,, but it didn't matter anyway ....because the jury members who were awake and the best ones who showed some sympathy were let go towards the end by the opposing lawyer and our lawyer!! Get this, the head of the jury was led by a woman paralegal from a local law firm so she could probably relate what the jurors were thinking and saying to her boss who could call our opposing lawyer and relate all to him.......so that is how probably they knew which members of the jury to dismiss! My lawyer at one time told me I was very jaded in my thinking...I wonder why? He also told me, I have the memory of an elephant, and I told him good memories evolve from truthful people, liars can't remember because their story is always changing!

Well, it was a five day session......however on Friday it ended early as they probably got rewarded a good lunch for screwing us as it ended in THEIR favor......we did not get a dime, nor justice from this case......and that is exactly what ALL involved wanted (both sides), they didn't dismiss the case, because I told them I would blow it loud and clear through-out the land......but they ALL knew if it LOOKED fair and was trial by jury....what could we say?? They WON......We still never found out who the Judge was that dismissed the lawyer's sons' three tickets, nor how much the two girls riding with the lawyers' son at the time of the accident in the back seat got for their settlement for their injuries. I'm sure the lawyers sons' girlfriends got some of our monies......they couldn't pay everyone, now could they? At the end of court, we asked our young lawyer what his father thought of the verdict? He said, "My father said great job son." That makes a lot of sense good job for losing the whole deal......Our opinion> someone got paid off!!!! What would you think?

This whole case of the first car accident took to settle>11 years!!

CHAPTER **13**

SECOND CAR ACCIDENT

Now, we had the second car accident to deal with and the man who hit us died about a year later from a disease he was battling with and from which he found out about around the time he hit us….

The opposing lawyer kept on telling us there would be a problem for a settlement because the man who hit us had died….I don't know why a problem would ensue……I told our lawyer, the man was covered by insurance and he was 100% negligent also, so there should be no problem at all……We were finally offered significant funds or so we thought, but there was never a make sense detailed write out of who got what and three (there is that magic number again) lawyers got paid out of our settlement even though we signed no payment unless they got us a settlement……now, I can see the last lawyer getting 1/3, but everyone else should NOT have gotten a cent!!!!

Will there ever be an end to this nightmare???

EPILOGUE……

Our prognosis……only time will tell.

Johnna has migraine headaches and other headaches every, every, day. She also has big time jaw problems with much pain. Her neck and back give her much trouble whenever she tries to do something or not! She acquired a permanent total disability acknowledged by four doctors.

I, Helen still have much pain in my left arm, which was my biggest complaint the minute the 1st car accident happened, I felt as if the life had went out of my arm and it did. That accident left me with a frozen shoulder, a torn rotator cuff, 3 bulging discs in my neck area, and torn ligaments in both my hands, upper back & neck pain and a broken elbow. The torn ligaments in both my hands required me to see a hand specialist who wanted to give me two new wrists! Thank goodness I am skeptical, I mentioned the wrist problem to my wonderful rheumatologist who assured me they would heal in time without surgery and they did (NOT his specialty>mind you)….three years of pain which kept me from many activities especially driving, so I had to get people to drive me > any and everywhere I had to go. Regarding the elbow problem, another bone/orthopedic doctor told me my elbow was shot and I needed a new elbow! However, a new elbow would bring misfortune, as it is a very risky procedure, not surgically performed much and the risk of infection is high, so I was told

EPILOGUE......

there is a possibility of losing my arm! Just as of late, my elbow/arm problems have escalated and now whatever I do, my elbow/arm area is giving me the sensation of catching and I cannot turn book pages very well or lift anything with that left arm without extreme pain or I end up dropping the item! Well, the possibility of surgery scares me half to death and as long as the elbow lasts, hopefully till I die> pain and all, I'll keep it as long as I can!

The small settlement helped somewhat monetarily from the 2nd car accident, but you can't live on air and with past money issues and bills that arose naturally through all the 12 years of our dilemma, it sure didn't help much with all the pain we deal with every day. I also sent a letter to the Judge and our lawyer who acquired this small settlement asking how much All four lawyers received individually......never an answer back from either one! Special gratitude to the wonderful father of my four daughters for his help> financially, emotionally, spiritually, physically and materially through our difficult time!

Things worked out with Compensation thanks to my lawyer and I have a permanent total disability verified by my doctors. I am also left with original left knee torn meniscus, right knee consequential torn meniscus which developed from overuse and RSD. A slight twist to the story regarding the f comp carrier girl I talked with from the beginning and had no sympathy whatsoever for me. I was told she ended up with a meniscus tear in her knee, so she wasn't there to torture people anymore on comp....thank goodness, I don't ever wish bad on people, but sometimes what goes around comes around.

All our injuries were evaluated by the best doctors in town regarding Johnna and myself! As I mentioned in the Twelfth Chapter, we ended up in the creek anyway and we should have walked out of Court that day....come what may?

SHUT UP HELEN

Poor, poor, Johnna ended up getting in three more car accidents after the first two with me, NOT her fault again with any! The Third One she was sitting in a cab in New York City and a city bus rear-ended the cab. Fourth One she was sitting in my car eating her lunch waiting for me to come back out from the store and a huge SUV backed into her, the woman claimed she never saw the car behind her with Johnna in it!! Fifth One, Johnna was stopped at a red stop light and an insurance man backed out from a parking spot here in town and backed into Johnna. When Johnna is afraid to pull out, when she was / is driving when there was a lot of traffic after she had been hit so many times...... I would say to her, "it's okay Johnna, they are NOT going to hit you, she would just look at me". I honestly think the poor girl has a target on her back!

At this time of the writing or finishing of this book......I am dealing with a left broken foot and walking with an air boot cast, because of babying my left knee, have caused a frontal overload on my toes/foot according to my foot specialists. The sad issue that really hurt me regarding these car accidents was when my ONLY granddaughter, my third daughter Darcy's daughter Alexis who was born in May of 2001...six months after our first car accident and because of my left arm problems... I didn't trust myself to hold her without sitting down first, so I wouldn't drop her, today's day, this year 2014 she will be thirteen years old. Now my granddaughter Alexis tells everyone how I go about saying ow, ow, ow constantly throughout the day and she is always saying poor, poor Grandma's elbow/arm.

I also am dealing now with problems from incompetent dentists throughout the years, fly-by-nights that have screwed up my teeth/mouth. Just for instance...... I was having trouble with an infection in my gum and I saw this dentist for the first time and after the hygienist took x-rays, she told her boss I had big time issues and the dentist told her I was doing fine. Well, the hygienist was so upset, she cleaned my teeth with such fervor and force that she loosened my caps and

EPILOGUE

when I went back, the dentist had let her go and needless to say I had let myself go also...... Another time, another dentist tried to remove a bridge in my mouth and couldn't get it off, so he wanted me to leave and come back another day with it loose and almost hanging, I told him I was not going anywhere, he was going to get it off right then... well he did and broke the tooth underneath and then my problems started.... So now looking for good dentists began? I thankfully found a wonderful dentist who is managing my mouth problem...you know I mean dental/teeth problems... Right? Also, as of late......going back to my R&L knee, my doctor sent a request for Hydrogel Shots which is a gel for the joints to help repair damaged cartilage and so can help you move somewhat better.... maybe, worth a try, so the request was put in months ago and denied. Now my doctor told me that comp NEVER denies these shots, oh yeah, but you're talking about me and my record!!!! The Comp Carrier wants me to try conventional means first BEFORE they approve these shots, conventional like anti-inflammatory medicine... which I already take, but bothers my stomach and they want to send me to therapy AGAIN which almost murdered my knees before with big time pain!!!!! The Saga Continues!!!! So, did I say END of Nightmare???? Oh Really!!

Oh no, please no more lawyers!!!!! SHUT UP HELEN!!!

I could go on and on with much more detail of all the crap we put up with from this Judicial System, but the book would be too big to carry and would stretch to the ends of the earth!

One thing we both developed was patience after 11-12 years......

PATIENCE IS A VIRTUE and sometimes VIRTUE REQUIRES PATIENCE

THE END
(Tentatively)

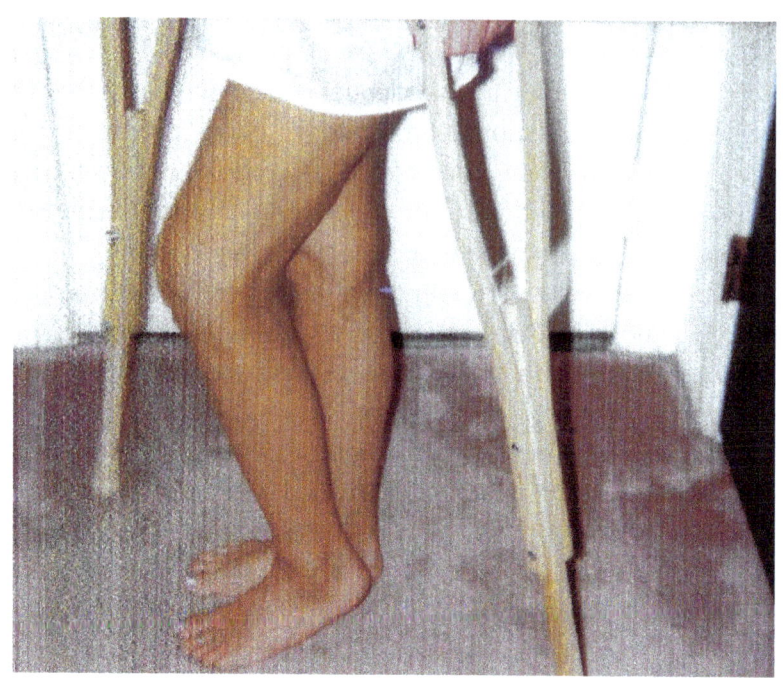

1999
My leg bent like a boomerang – could not straighten it!

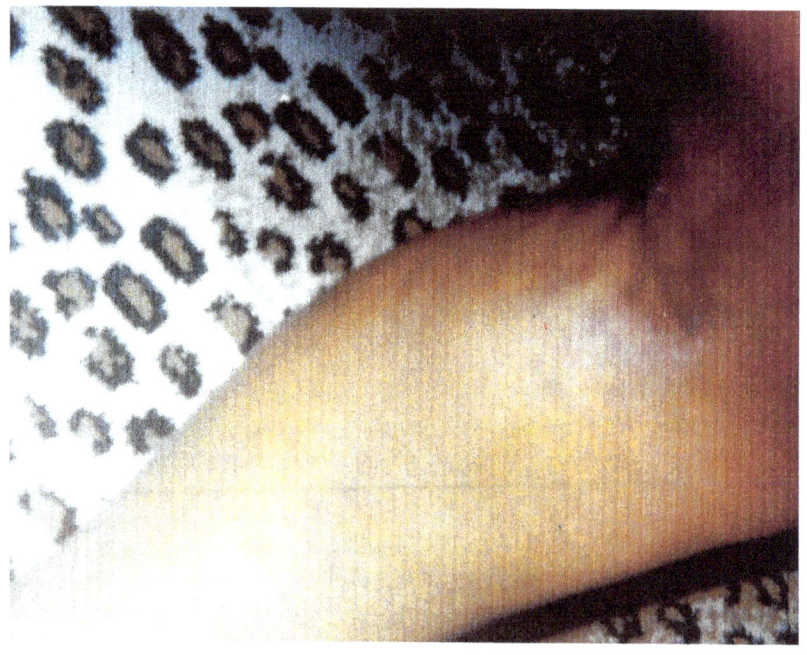

1999
My leg bent like a boomerang – could not straighten it!

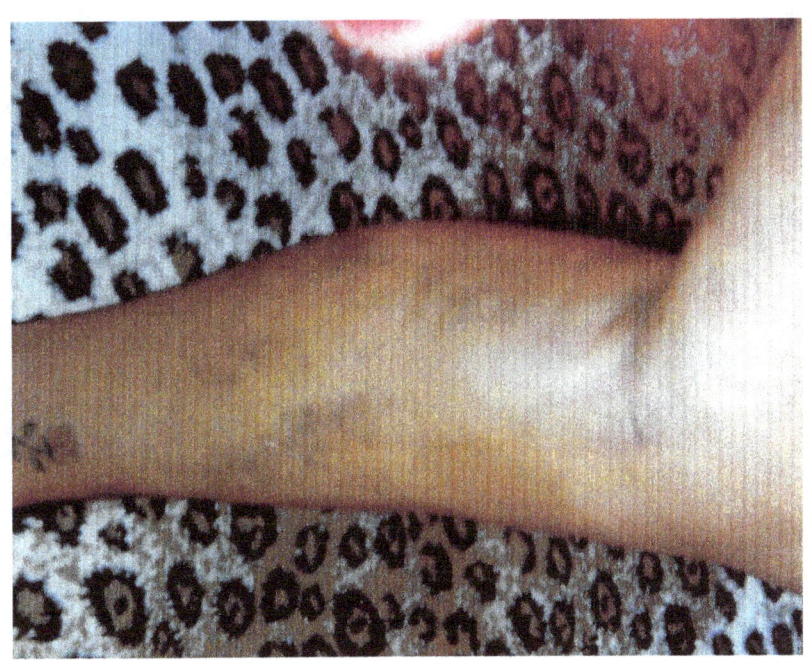

1999
My leg bent like a boomerang – could not straighten it!

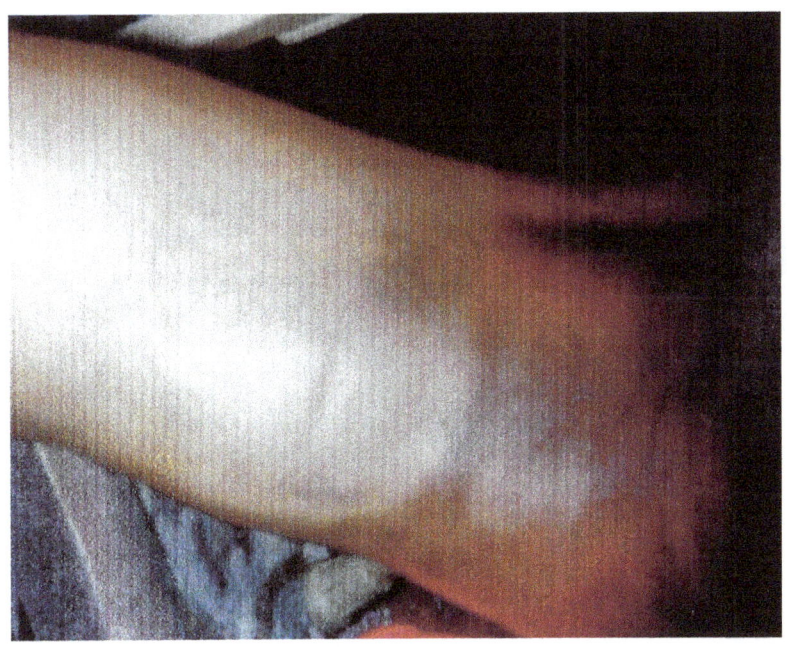

1999
Leg – black + blue

November 2000
Totaled car pictures from "1st" car accident.

November 2000
Totaled car pictures from "1st" car accident.

November 2000
Totaled car pictures from "1st" car accident.

November 2000
Totaled car pictures from "1st" car accident.

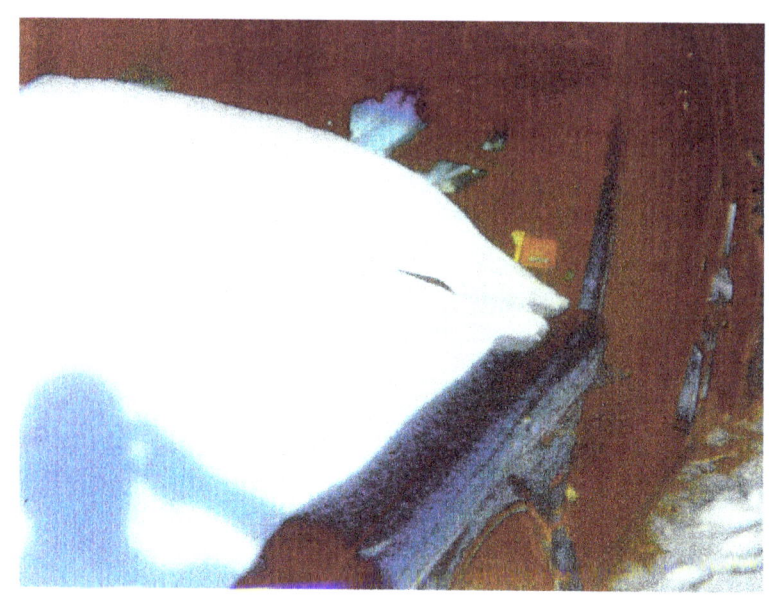

November 2000
Totaled car pictures from "1st" car accident.

November 2000
Totaled car pictures from "1st" car accident.

November 2000
Totaled car pictures from "1st" car accident.

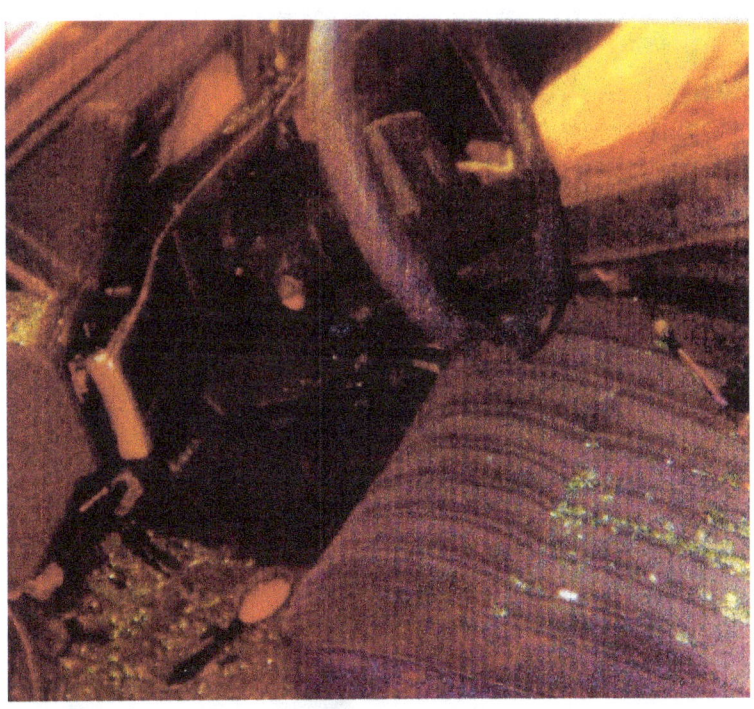

November 2000
Totaled car pictures from "1st" car accident.

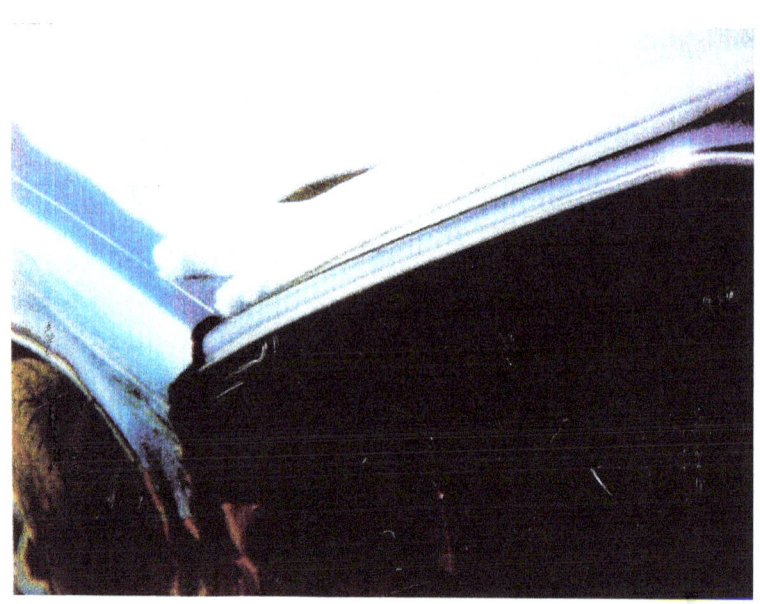

*November 2000
Totaled car pictures from "1st" car accident.*

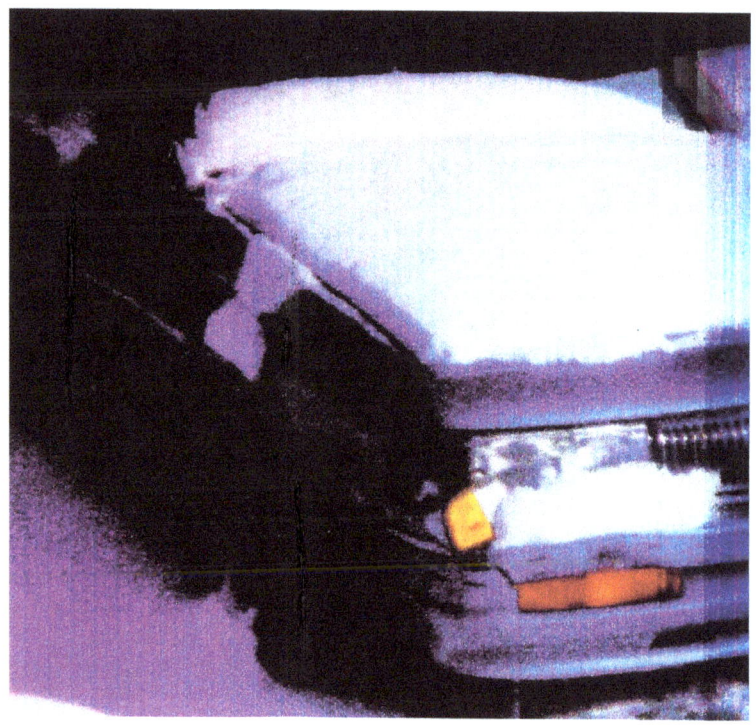

*November 2000
Totaled car pictures from "1st" car accident.*

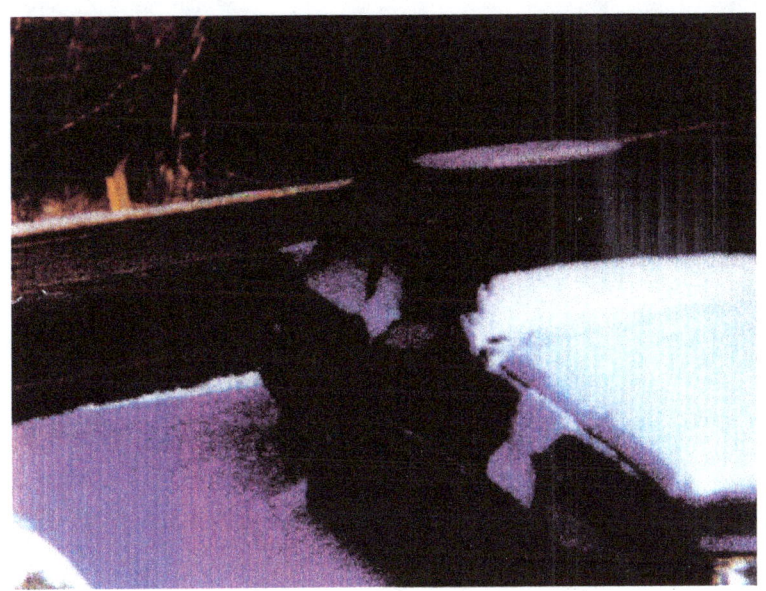

November 2000
Totaled car pictures from "1st" car accident.

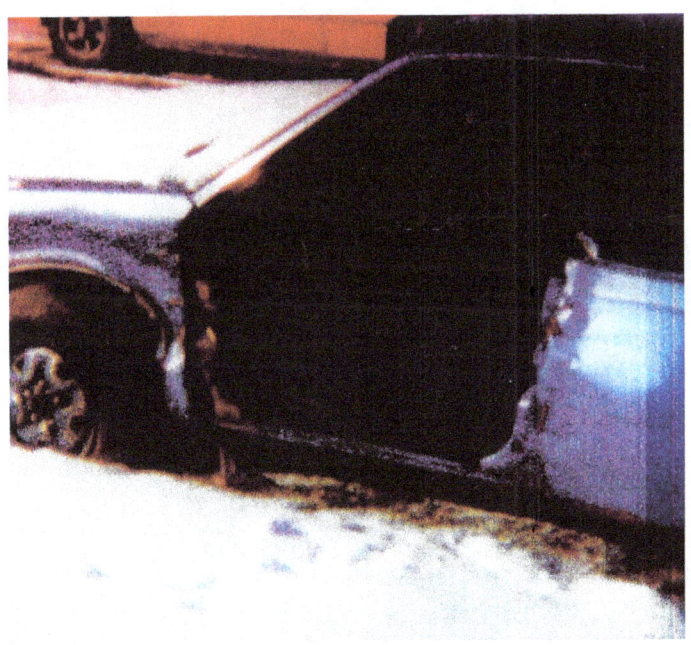

November 2000
Totaled car pictures from "1st" car accident.

November 2000
Totaled car pictures from "1st" car accident.

November 2000
Totaled car pictures from "1st" car accident.

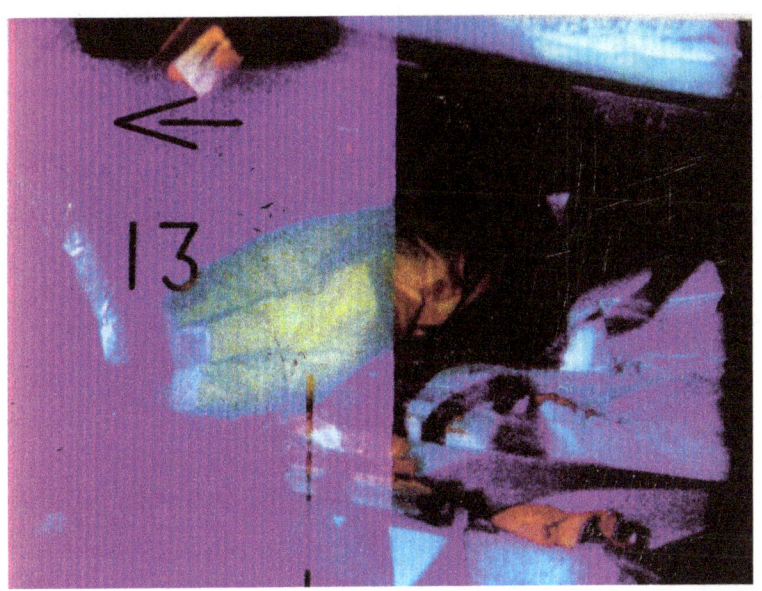

November 2000
Totaled car pictures from "1st" car accident.

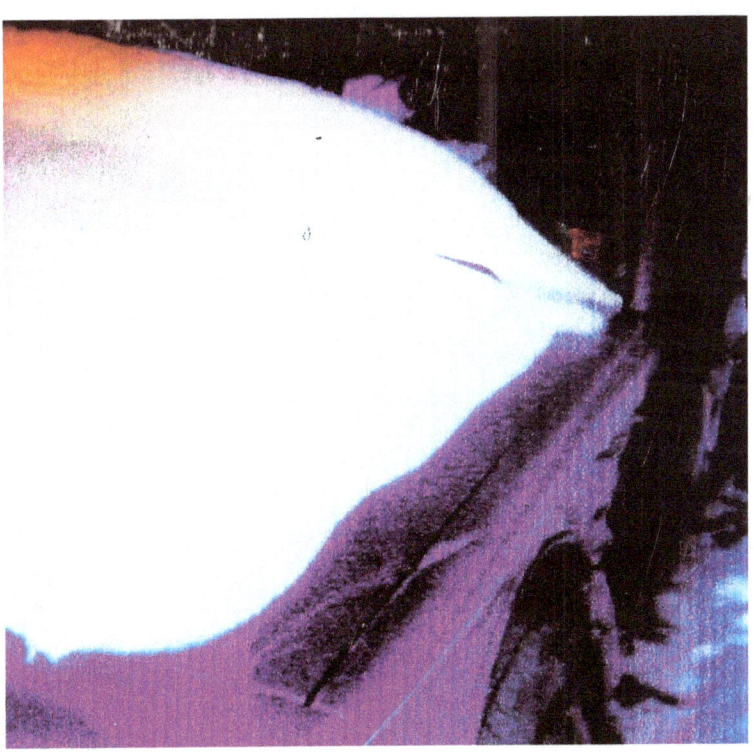

November 2000
Totaled car pictures from "1st" car accident.

www.ingramcontent.com/pod-product-compliance
Lightning Source LLC
Chambersburg PA
CBHW061516040426
42450CB00008B/1652